THE CRAB ALPHABET BOOK

JERRY PALLOTTA

ILLUSTRATED BY TOM LEONARD

iꞮꞮi Charlesbridge

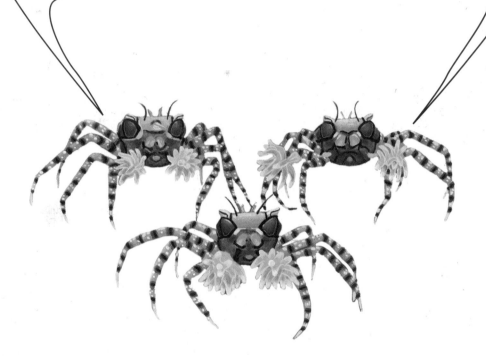

A big Peggotty Beach thank-you to mosser K. F. McDonald, bailer Kathie Mac, and air-traffic controller Kate Hale. —J.P.

In memory of my father-in-law, James Drew (1929–2013). "March on, good soldier." —T.L.

DEAR READER,
We crabs are tired of books about cute penguins, proud tigers, colorful butterflies, and other favorite animals. What about us? We believe it's time for our very own book. We hope you'll enjoy it! Sincerely,

THE CRABS
(The coolest, crustiest creatures on earth)

Published by Charlesbridge
85 Main Street
Watertown, MA 02472
(617) 926-0329
www.charlesbridge.com

Library of Congress Cataloging-in-Publication Data

Names: Pallotta, Jerry, author. | Leonard, Thomas, 1955- illustrator.
Title: The crab alphabet book / Jerry Pallotta; illustrated by Tom Leonard.
Other titles: Crab alphabet
Description: Watertown, MA : Charlesbridge, [2019]
Identifiers: LCCN 2017056279| ISBN 9781570911446 (reinforced for library use) | ISBN 9781570911484 (pbk.) | ISBN 9781632898012 (ebook pdf) | ISBN 9781632898005 (e-book)
Subjects: LCSH: Crabs—Juvenile literature. | English language—Alphabet—Juvenile literature. | Alphabet books.
Classification: LCC QL444.M33 P3527 2019 | DDC 595.3/86—dc23
LC record available at https://lccn.loc.gov/2017056279

Printed in China
(hc) 10 9 8 7 6 5 4 3 2 1
(sc) 10 9 8 7 6 5 4 3 2 1

Illustrations done in acrylic paint on illustration board
Display type set in Core Circus by S-Core, Co., Ltd.
Text type set in Mikado by Hannes von Döhren
Sidebar type set in Providence Bold by Guy Jeffrey Nelson, FontShop International
Color separations by Colourscan Print Co Pte Ltd, Singapore
Printed by 1010 Printing International Limited in Huizhou, Guangdong, China
Production supervision by Brian G. Walker
Designed by Joyce White

A is for **Arrow Crab.** This skinny creature with the arrow-shaped head and body is an ocean crab. Some crabs live in water, and some live on land. All crabs need water to survive.

Aa

All crabs are decapods. The scientific word decapod means "ten feet." Crabs have eight legs and two claws. Eight plus two equals ten.

Bb

Crabs belong to a group of animals called crustaceans. All crustaceans have a hard, crusty shell and two pairs of antennae.

B is for **Blue Crab**. Look at its pair of back legs, which are shaped like paddles. The blue crab is a swimming crab, but it can also run fast. When blue crabs get loose on fishing boats, crab fishermen yell, "Biter in the boat! Biter in the boat!"

C is for **Christmas Island Crab**. These crabs live mainly on land. At the beginning of the rainy season, millions migrate to the ocean to lay their eggs. Moving down hills, through trees, and over roads, these crabs just keep on coming, like in a scary movie. Their amazing red migration can be seen from an airplane.

Dd

D is for **Decorator Crab.** A decorator crab hides by covering its shell. This crab has covered itself in purple seaweed. It's well camouflaged and difficult to find. If this crab lived among green seaweed, it would wear green.

Ee

E is for **Elbow Crab**. It's easy to see how this crab got its name. It has extremely long claws. It holds food in its elbows.

Crabs have a protective shell on the outside of their bodies. It is called an exoskeleton.

Ff

F is for **Fiddler Crab.**
Male fiddler crabs have one
giant claw and one tiny claw.
Females' claws are both the
same size. Claws are also
called pincers.

Fiddler crabs shoot
spitballs. They scoop
mud and sand into
their mouth, swallow
whatever is edible, and
then spit out the rest.
Don't try this at the
dinner table!

G is for **Ghost Crab.** Ghost crabs dig deep burrows in the sand to hide from the hot sun. You can see their entrance holes as you walk along a beach. Ghost crabs are nocturnal—active only at night. When the sun goes down, they wake up, leave their tunnels, and can surprise people.

Gg

Most crabs have eyes like periscopes. They can raise and lower their eyes and turn them one way and the other to see all around.

Hh

H is for **Halloween Crab**. Wouldn't it be funny if you found a Halloween crab on Easter Island? This crab's black and orange colors remind people of Halloween.

Human beings have red, iron-based blood. Crabs have bluish-green, copper-based blood.

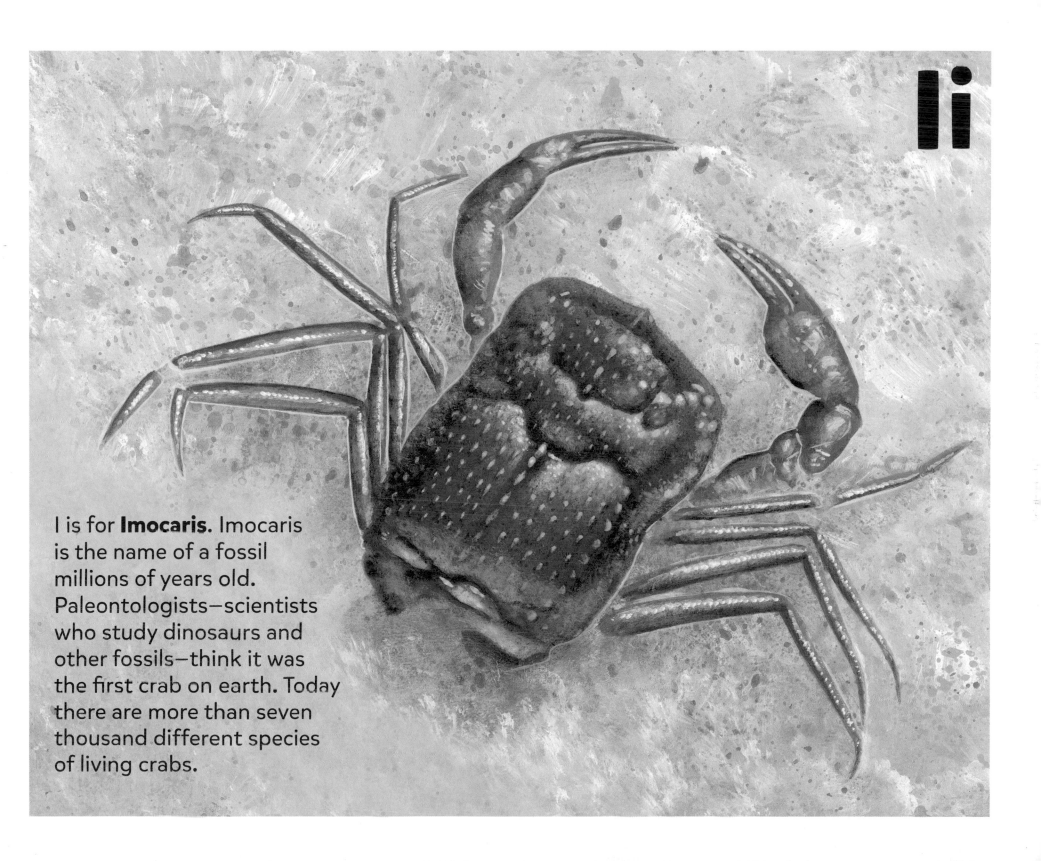

I is for **Imocaris**. Imocaris is the name of a fossil millions of years old. Paleontologists—scientists who study dinosaurs and other fossils—think it was the first crab on earth. Today there are more than seven thousand different species of living crabs.

Jj

J is for **Japanese Spider Crab**.
This is the longest crab in the world. Its legs can be more than six feet long. Wow! Including its body, that's up to thirteen feet across. The Japanese spider crab might be the world's greatest mountain climber. It can climb the walls of underwater terrain.

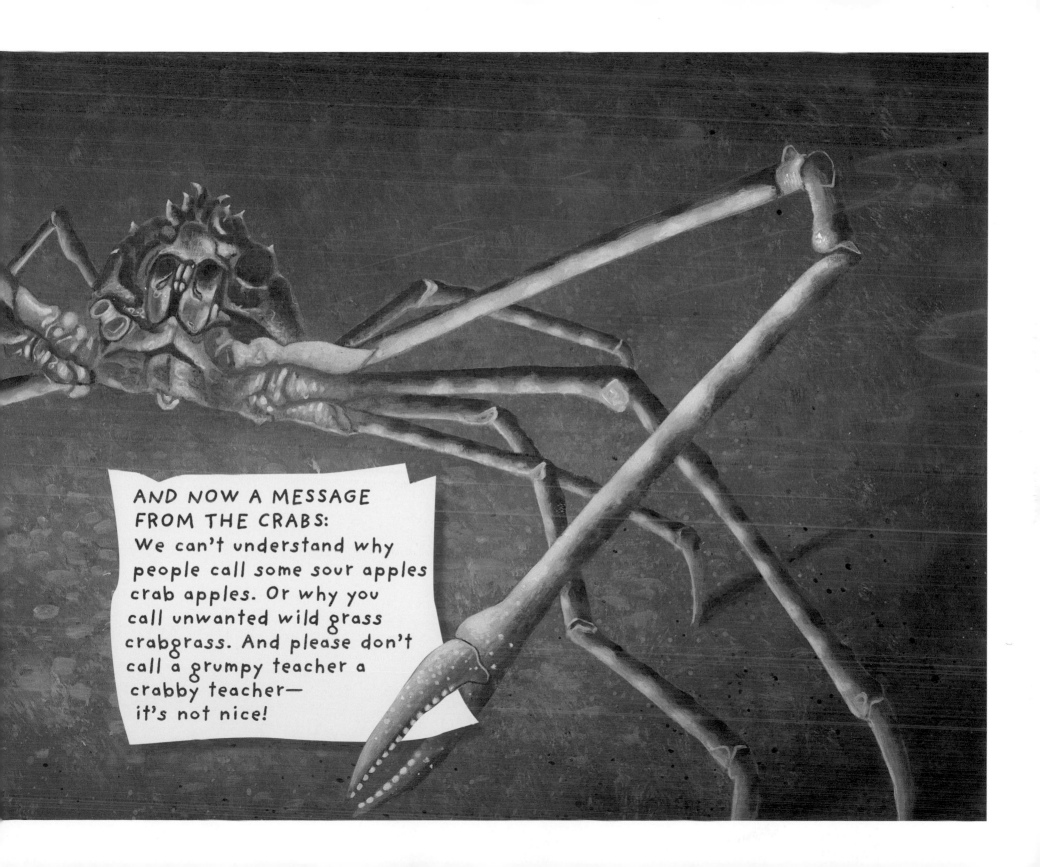

Kk

K is for **King Crab**. Many people love to eat seafood. Tons of king crab are served in restaurants worldwide. Crabbers catch them with crab traps, fishing nets, and trotlines. Harvesting crabs and other shellfish such as lobsters, clams, and shrimp is a major industry.

L is for **Little Green Crab**.
The best time to find little
green crabs is at low tide. Gently
pick up a rock, look in a beach
puddle, or peek under seaweed,
and you might spot some.

Exploring nature at low tide
along the shoreline is called
tidepooling.

LI

Mm

M is for **Mitten Crab**. Is this crab wearing mittens? Mitten crabs have a shell like other crabs, but they also have bristles that look like fur on their claws. Hairy claws are an unusual trait.

How do crabs grow larger? They molt. Molting occurs when a crab sheds its shell and grows a new, bigger one. This mitten crab has just molted.

N is for **Ninja Crab**. In Japan, it is also called samurai crab or Heikegani. Some people think the back of this crab looks like the face of a ninja warrior. Other people believe that ninja crabs may be their dead ancestors. The "face" on these crabs spooks some fishermen, who refuse to hurt these crabs.

Oo

O is for **Oyster Crab**. Oyster crabs are members of the pea crab family, which are considered the world's smallest crabs. They often live inside clams, mussels, and oysters. President George Washington liked to see pea crabs floating in his oyster stew.

Maybe someday you will become a carcinologist—a scientist who studies crabs and other crustaceans—and discover an even smaller crab!

P is for **Pom Pom Crab**. It holds venomous anemones in its claws. This crab may look like a cheerleader, but it packs a punch! It holds the anemones like boxing gloves and punches predators.

Get away, hungry fish!

P p

Qq

Q is for **Queen Crab**. When delicious king crabs became overfished, commercial crabbers and restaurant owners started selling Tanner crabs. To make Tanner crabs more popular with diners, they were renamed queen crabs. In some restaurants, they are called snow crabs.

R is for **Robber Crab.** Thief! Thief! This is the world's largest and heaviest land crab. If you are on an island with robber crabs, keep an eye on your belongings. Robber crabs steal things. Oops, your lunch is missing. Don't forget to look up—robber crabs can climb trees. They are also called coconut crabs.

Rr

S is for **Soldier Crab**. Most crabs walk sideways. The soldier crab walks straight ahead just like a soldier. At low tide, it is common for these crabs to march like an army to the ocean. *Attention! Forward march! Hup, two, three, four!*

Ss

S could also be for **Sea Spider**. Sea spiders are not spiders, and they are not crabs! They look strange. Could they be aliens from another planet? At first, scientists didn't know how to classify them. Now we know they are closer relations to spiders than crabs.

Tt

If a crab loses a claw or a leg, it grows back. Regeneration, or the growing back of a lost limb, is rare in the animal world.

T is for **Thorn-legged Crab**. This crab's thorny shell and legs offer protection from predators. Its thorny body is tough for predators to swallow.

Uu

U is for **Urchin Crab.** The urchin crab defends itself by carrying a sea urchin— a spiny creature—on its back. This crab walks on four of its legs and carries the urchin with its other legs. Clever!

V is for **Velvet Crab**. This crab is pregnant. The bulge on its tail is thousands of crab eggs. Pregnant crabs are called eggers, spongers, or berried crabs. When her eggs hatch, this mom will have thousands of baby crabs. She is lucky she doesn't have to buy shoes for her kids.

Vv

Ww

W is for **Wrinkled Crab**. This crab has a carapace that is ridged, or wrinkled. A crab's one-piece top shell is called its carapace. Carapaces can be smooth, bumpy, spiky, or many other textures and colors. Look at all the different kinds in this book!

X is for **Xeno Crab**. Its full scientific name is *Xenocarcinus depressus*. Crabs live in different habitats—rain forests, muddy bottoms, sandy shoals, rocks and jetties, marshlands, shipwrecks, deep water, shallow creeks, kelp forests, fishing banks, and even the Sargasso Sea. You can find a xeno crab in a tropical coral reef.

Yy

Y is for **Yeti Crab**. This fuzzy crab has no eyes. It is named after the Yeti, a cryptid. A cryptid is an animal that people search for, but have not yet found. Yeti, Bigfoot, Mokèlé-mbèmbé, Nessie, Bessie, and Chessie are all cryptids. You can discover more about these legendary creatures at your library!

Z is for **Zebra Hermit Crab**. Hermit crabs have a hard covering on their legs and claws, but their body is soft. To protect themselves, hermit crabs live in the discarded shells of other animals. This zebra hermit crab has found a nice home in a snail shell.

Zz

DEAR READER,

Thank you for reading about us cool crabs. This creature is a horseshoe crab. But don't be fooled! It has "crab" in its name, but is not a crab. Horseshoe crabs are more closely related to scorpions. The horseshoe crab's mouth is between its legs! We hope to see you at the beach, and remember—we didn't want our own book because we're selfish. We're shellfish!

—THE CRABS